HOW TO BE SCHOOL SMART

Elizabeth James & Carol Barkin

HOW TO BE SCHOOL SMART

Secrets of Successful Schoolwork

Pictures by Roy Doty

With an introduction by
M. JEAN GREENLAW, Ph.D.

Lothrop, Lee & Shepard Books   New York

First Edition 1 2 3 4 5 6 7 8 9 10

Library of Congress Cataloging in Publication Data
James, Elizabeth. How to Be School Smart.
Includes index. Summary: Discusses a variety of simple techniques for devel-
oping effective study habits. 1. Study, Method of—Juvenile literature.
2. Homework—Juvenile literature. 3. Students—Time management—
Juvenile literature. [1. Study, Method of. 2. Homework]
I. Barkin, Carol. II. Doty, Roy, 1922–   , ill. III. Title.
LB1601.5.J36   1988
371.3'028'1   87-2899
ISBN 0-688-06798-0 (pbk.)
ISBN 0-688-06799-9 (lib. bdg.)

For Elsa DeVita and all the others
who shared their knowledge
and expertise with us

Contents

To the Student

Have you ever felt panic when your teacher announced a test was coming? Have you ever lost or forgotten to do your homework? Or maybe you read an assignment and then couldn't remember the important points when it came time to report in class. If you are someone who would like to learn to be organized and to be more successful in your school assignments and tests, then *How to be School Smart* is the book for you.

James and Barkin begin by explaining the need for a regular study space and giving you suggestions for establishing it. They help you select an appropriate space in your home and stock it with all the materials necessary for good studying. They even give suggestions for setting a mood for studying.

Once you have selected an appropriate space, you need to concentrate on organizing your time. The first task is to discover how you *really* spend your time each day, which you can do by making a time chart. The results might surprise you! Then you can begin to plan how to organize your days, weeks, and even months. The authors point out that this is not meant to make you a slave to work, but to help give you more time to accomplish your tasks and more time for fun, too.

Have you ever noticed that you don't learn things the same way a friend or family member does? This is not unusual, and an important key to performing well in school is to discover the way you learn best. James and

Barkin discuss the various learning styles and suggestions for studying in a way that takes advantage of *your* learning style.

Homework can be viewed as a chance to practice and to polish what you have learned in school as well as an opportunity to explore ideas on your own. This book includes advice on how to produce homework that will increase your understanding and please your teacher.

Taking tests is an important part of school. The authors give very specific examples of how to study for a test, how to get into a good frame of mind to take the test, and how to make an overview of the test to produce your best plan of attack. They then provide suggestions for answering typical types of questions such as essays and true-false.

How to Be School Smart is both useful and enjoyable. Ideas are presented clearly and precise examples are supplied. The book should help anyone become a better-prepared student.

I highly recommend this book to students, as you are the ones most responsible for seeing that you succeed in school. It is also useful to parents and teachers who can help students get the most from the school experience.

M. JEAN GREENLAW
Regents Professor
North Texas State University

HOW TO BE
SCHOOL
SMART

1. Steps to Success

What do you want in school? How about straight A's on your report card and a way to learn everything you need to know quickly and easily? Probably everyone you know wants school to be like this. But no one thinks it can actually happen.

Of course, no method of approaching schoolwork can guarantee that you will get straight A's. But the ideas in this book really will help you learn to study more efficiently and to take tests without panicking. You'll be able to organize yourself and find time for all your homework, as well as for the other things you want to do. You'll discover the style of learning that works best for you so you can make the most of your study time. And you'll relax about tests and quizzes once you master the tips and hints revealed in these pages.

As you get older and move up through the grades in school, it's exciting to find new areas of knowledge opening up to you. But sometimes it can be kind of confusing and even a little scary. Probably you have more homework now than ever before; often you may feel as if you don't know where to begin. And when you're faced with difficult tests, you may get so worried that you can't even think.

This book will help! The ideas and techniques in these pages will allow you to focus on doing your best work at home and in class. When you uncover the terrific student you truly are, you'll have a head start on success in school.

2. Organizing Your Study Space

"You've got to get organized!" How many times have you told yourself that, or had someone else say it to you? It sounds like a good idea, but it's not always so easy to do. How can you get started?

Most people feel that it's helpful to have a special place where you do your studying. The idea is to train your brain so that every time you plop down in your study space, your mind clicks in and says, "Time to study!"

Your study space may not be exactly like someone else's. If you have your own bedroom, your study space might be in one corner, with a desk, a chair, and a bulletin board. What if you share a room with a younger brother or sister who goes to bed early? Maybe you can make a study space somewhere else in the house, like the family room or the breakfast nook. Ask your mom and dad for suggestions. Even a card table that you set up in the living room every afternoon can be a perfectly fine study space.

Essential equipment

What does your study space need to contain? First, good light. Whatever kind of homework you are doing, you need light that makes it easy to see the work and doesn't make you squint. Some people like to have a lot of light when they study. Are you someone who turns on the overhead light in the room and all the lamps as well? Or do you prefer a less bright room and a warm pool of light from your reading lamp? Try to arrange the lighting in your study space the way you like it—you'll get more work done.

Second, you need a surface—a desk or a table—to write on. Writing on a book balanced in your lap almost guarantees sloppy penmanship, and it's tiring because your arm is held in an awkward position.

Third, your homework materials need to be available while you study. Pencils, pens, scratch paper, and good paper, as well as your textbooks and assignments, are all important—without them it's hard to do your work! In addition, you may need special equipment. If you're working on geometry, don't leave your protractor and compass at school.

Is your study space also used by other members of your family—for eating, TV watching, or whatever? If it is, you should have an easy method of moving your things out of the way when you're finished studying for the day. Try using a sturdy cardboard box that's big enough to hold all your equipment. Decorate it with stickers or a collage and add your name in big bold letters. You can keep the box under your bed and then you'll always know where to find it.

Extras

There are lots of extras that are not strictly necessary for your study space but might be nice to have. Perhaps you already own a dictionary. This reference book is probably the most useful one for any student. You can use it to check the correct spelling of a word or to find out exactly what it means. But did you know that dictionaries also give examples of how a specific word can be used in a sentence? And they list synonyms (words with the same or similar meaning) for the word you're looking up.

Another handy reference tool is an atlas. The very large ones you see in libraries are quite expensive, but a smaller version in paperback is great to have. In addition to maps of countries and continents, it may give other types of information about population, natural resources, climate, and so on.

If you can put up a bulletin board in your study space, you'll find it very convenient. Where else can you tack up that list of people who are working on the science project with you, and what each of them is supposed to be doing? The great thing about a bulletin board is that what's pinned on it doesn't have to stay there forever—when you're finished with something, you can take it down and throw it away.

Setting the mood

Are you the type who likes to have the radio going in the background while you're doing your homework? Or do you prefer peace and quiet? Experts who study how people learn are convinced that there are different types of study habits. It appears that some students can concentrate best when there are no noises at all to distract them. Others, however, seem to need a steady flow of background sound to help them think. It may be that music on the radio blocks out other sounds such as traffic noises or people calling to one another.

It's not hard to experiment to figure out which type you are. Trying studying both ways and see what works best for you. Don't use this as an excuse to listen to your favorite DJ instead of studying! But if you really do get more done with the radio burbling quietly nearby, point this out to your mom next time she tells you to "turn it off so you can concentrate." She may need some convincing if she's the type who prefers peace and quiet—it's up to you to prove your point by getting terrific grades on your homework.

Watching television while you study is another matter, though. You need to have your eyes on your work and not on the flickering screen. And it's hard to keep yourself from getting caught up in a show that's on. If you do get drawn into the show, you'll find that you can hardly remember a thing from the chapter you thought you were reading.

It's interesting to see some of the other differences in the ways people like to study. Some find it best to sit in a straight-backed chair at a table or desk to read—they find they learn more this way. But others prefer to lounge on a bed or curl up in an armchair while reading a chapter or two. Such people may change position often, and it's possible that moving around helps them concentrate.

No one knows for sure why these variations in study patterns exist. But finding out how you work best is one step on the way to doing better in school.

Keep clutter under control

Here's another difference among people. Are you the type who puts every baseball card or china figurine away neatly in its own special spot every time? Or do you find yourself rooting around on the closet floor for the one comic book or computer game you're sure must be there somewhere?

Super-organized people are really lucky. They don't have to work at keeping their things neat and ready whenever they're needed, and this can be a big asset in handling schoolwork. But what about the rest of us who may seem totally disorganized?

Don't let this worry you too much. Keep in mind that what looks like a mess to someone else may be a perfectly okay system of organization for you. It's not necessary to have everything you own filed in special folders and arranged in alphabetical order. You just have to be able to find the things you need when you need them.

One easy way to keep track of all your stuff is to stash it in cardboard boxes. Here's how to do it:

Clear off a large section of the floor and begin making piles of various things. Homework that's been handed back but that should be kept for review goes in one pile. Materials for a research project or paper go in another pile. Bits of paper you can't bear to throw out (last year's birthday cards, the flyer from the amusement park you went to this summer, a photo of a bird from a magazine) are collected in a third pile. You get the idea. And of course, some things can go directly into the wastebasket.

Now look for boxes the right size for these various things you want to keep. For small things (like tapes, box tops you're saving up to send away, postcards, and the little oddments that accumulate on top of your dresser), shoeboxes are perfect. For papers, try to find a box that typing paper or file folders came in, or a shirt-size box from a department store. A local store may have extra boxes to give away if you ask.

Once everything is neatly sorted and boxed,

it's a good idea to label each box. That way you'll remember what to put where, and you'll be reminded when you see the label that that's the box for your homework papers or basketball flyers or whatever.

You'll want to keep your boxes where you can get at them easily. Stacking them on a bookshelf is great. But if you don't have an empty shelf, think about other spaces that would work. What about the floor of your closet, next to your desk, or under your bed? Anyplace that is handy to reach will work fine.

Get the good out of it!

Now that you've gotten your study space all put together the way you want it, go ahead and use it. There you are at your desk—your pencils in a Mickey Mouse mug from Disneyland, all your papers close at hand, and your reading light turned on. Sitting in the spot you've created for schoolwork definitely puts you more in the mood to do it. Now you're ready to tackle anything.

3. Organizing Your Time

Maybe you feel as if your time is already a lot more organized than you'd like. You've got to go to school every morning, then get to your piano lesson or baseball practice, be home in time to do your chores before dinner, and still have your homework done before you can watch TV. Sometimes it seems as if there isn't time to do everything, and people are always telling you to hurry and not to be late.

On Tuesday and Thursday afternoons, however, Bill has to be at soccer practice by 4:30. It will probably take him about twenty minutes to change into his shorts and team T-shirt and run to the practice field. That leaves him forty minutes of free time. How could he use it best? Perhaps that's long enough to do a spelling review or to finish most of his math assignment. On the other hand, it might be better for Bill to use that forty minutes to walk the dog and practice his music.

But wait a minute! This Tuesday he doesn't have that forty minutes before soccer practice—he'll be on the way home from the dentist's office. And besides, he has a big spelling test on Wednesday that he wants to study for. How would you solve a similar problem? Maybe Bill will be able to squeeze in some homework time during lunch on Tuesday, or he could get up extra early Wednesday morning.

Like Bill, you may find it hard to fit in all your activities, but it's also fun to arrange your schedule so it makes more sense. When you've filled in your own time chart for the coming week, pin it up on the bulletin board or your door so you can see what you're supposed to be doing each day.

How is your plan working?

Now you get to do the most interesting part of the time chart. Save yourself five or ten minutes at the end of each day and fill out another copy of your time chart with the things you *really* did that day. You might be amazed at how different your two charts look by the end of the week!

Be as honest as you can when you write down what you actually spent your time on. No one is going to see this schedule but you, and you won't be graded on it. On pages 24–25 you can see what Bill did during his week, and you can compare it to what he had planned to do.

When you compare your plan with what you ended up doing, you may find places where they don't match up at all. Don't get upset about this—most people plan to do more than is humanly possible. But by comparing the two charts, you can learn a lot about your study habits. You may see how to use your time in a way that works better for you.

Another thing your time charts can show you is how much time you spend fooling around. Bill had looked forward to the movie at the library on Sunday. But when that time rolled around, he hadn't done any of the work for his term paper. Looking over his week, you can see how it happened.

Everyone needs some time for just fooling around—no one can or should plan to work all the time. But maybe you can adjust your schedule so you'll get the most good out of your free time. For example, Bill might decide that he's been goofing off too much in the afternoons. Maybe he could eat an apple while he walks the dog—then he'd be able to get down to studying at 4:00. And it worked well to practice his music right after dinner, so maybe he'll plan it that way for next week. Then he'll have time for a movie over the weekend.

The whole point of finding out what you actually do every hour for a whole week is to learn what works and doesn't work for you. With this in mind, you can plan your time according to your personal "internal clock" instead of trying to force yourself to fit someone else's pattern.

Try keeping time charts for yourself for two

or three weeks. By then you'll have learned a lot about your own study habits. Maybe you'll find you're getting more done in less time, or that you're not spending so much time worrying about work that isn't done. Later on, if you start to feel disorganized again, you can begin keeping weekly charts until you get back on track.

Looking at the big picture

Another terrific tool to help keep your time organized is a large monthly calendar. Try to find the kind that is used as a desk blotter; these usually measure at least $1\frac{1}{2} \times 2$ feet. They are made like a pad of paper, and you tear off each month when it is finished. There is a large square for each day, so it's easy to write down the things you need to remember.

Hang the calendar on the wall or lay it flat on your desk—just make sure to keep it somewhere handy so you'll look at it every day.

The idea is to enter all the important events that are coming up in the next month. The due date for a term paper, the days when tests will be given, and the times of parties or athletic events can all be noted on this big calendar. If you have a part-time job, like baby-sitting or yard work, be sure to make a note of those times, too. Then you'll be able to look ahead and get an idea of how to arrange your study time and your social time.

If you look around at the people you know, you'll notice that most busy adults keep a monthly calendar. It lets them know what's coming up and helps them feel in control of their lives. It can do the same thing for you! Making notes of what's going to happen and glancing at them every day or two will keep you from being surprised by that midterm test and will remind you to get going on the science project or term paper you have to turn in next month.

As you get in the habit of using a calendar to keep track of what's happening, jotting down notes of future events will become almost automatic. You'll feel that you know what you're doing and you'll be amazed at how much you accomplish. Besides, it's fun to decide how to use all that extra time you've saved!

4. Different Ways of Learning

There are many different ways to learn things, and most of these ways are used in school. Does this surprise you? Think about it. In school you learn by reading words in books; by looking at or "reading" picture languages like maps, graphs, and charts; by listening to and watching films and film strips; by listening to teachers talk; by making displays or dioramas; by typing on a computer and reading what appears on the screen; by doing experiments that demonstrate ideas; by writing down spelling words and math calculations; by writing essays that explain your ideas; by memorizing poems or lists of words in another language. You can probably think of other ways you learn.

People who study education have done research about different "learning styles." It seems that there are three main ways that people learn things: by seeing (which includes reading), by hearing, and by touching or working with things.

How do you learn best?

Most people use all their senses to learn things, and they don't learn in only one way. But some students find that they learn better in one way than in others. It can be very helpful to know which learning styles work best for you.

Perhaps you already know something about how you learn best. Do you remember things best if you hear them explained out loud in words? Or do you do better if you read those things in a book? Some people feel they really know something only if they pick up a pen and write it down themselves.

Think about how you learn new spelling words. Are you the type of student who memorizes the way words are spelled by looking at them? Or do you remember the way the letters are arranged by spelling the words out loud? Or perhaps the easiest way for you to be sure you are ready for a spelling test is to write each new word down a couple of times. And it's possible that you prefer two or even all three of these ways of learning.

Tricks for better reading

Reading is perhaps the most important skill for doing well in school. It seems that you are always reading, not only for language arts but also for social studies, science, even math.

Sometimes when you're faced with studying a big section of text, you may feel as though you can't remember a thing you read. There are tricks for getting the most out of the pages you are supposed to read and understand.

Look before you leap!

Many of the books you read for school have lots of headings and other guideposts to learning. Chapter titles and subtitles, section summaries, questions to think about, marginal notes, and captions for pictures, graphs, and maps are all helpful tools for you to use.

Before you begin your actual reading assignment, take time to page through your book and look at titles, headings, and summaries. Many chapters have introductions, and these are worth reading. An introduction tells you in short form what you are about to learn when you read that chapter.

The people who write textbooks want to help you learn. Take advantage of the clues they provide about the material you are going to read. One of these clues is the kind of type used in the headings and subheadings. The most important topics usually have headings in larger type or in darker type, called boldface. Reading them will let you know what the chapter is about.

Textbooks often have a list of questions at the beginning or end of each chapter. Take a

look at the questions before you read the
chapter. Reading them out loud to yourself
might help fix them in your mind. The questions will give you an idea of what kinds of
information you will be expected to know after
you've finished reading the material. Keep
these questions in mind as you read and the
answers will probably leap right off the page
at you!

Read it your way

Reading for a school subject is not quite the
same as reading a novel for fun. After reading
a class assignment, you are expected to remember the information and to be able to join
in a class discussion. Sometimes it's hard to
keep all those facts and ideas in your head,
but there are ways to make it easier. Why not
use your knowledge of learning styles to come
up with a method that works well for you?

THE EYES HAVE IT

If you learn best by reading, a good way to
make sure you understand a chapter is to go

back over the headings and questions. As you read each heading and subheading, think about what information that section contains. Then, when you reread the questions, see if you can give a good answer to each one. You may find that you remember what part of the chapter the answer comes from; you may even "see" the words on the page in your mind's eye.

LET'S HEAR IT

If you learn best by listening, a tape recorder is a handy tool. Try reading the entire chapter onto the tape and then listening to it. This way you hear it twice. Or you might find that it's just as effective to take taped notes as you read. After reading each short section, read its heading out loud and then give a short verbal summary of what that section contains.

Once you've read the whole assignment, read the questions from the book onto your tape and give an answer to each in your own words. Be sure to look back through the chapter to check any facts you're not sure of.

Every time you listen to your tape, it's like reading the information all over again, so these tapes will be very helpful when you are reviewing for a test. Just be sure to label each tape clearly with the book and chapter titles as well as the date. Then you can easily find the parts you need to review. When you've taken your final test in that class, you can erase the tape and use it for another subject.

REACH OUT AND TOUCH IT

Maybe you have discovered you learn best through your senses of touch and movement. In that case, you will want to write down notes as you read through your material. The act of picking up a pencil and shaping the words helps many people remember facts and ideas.

Keep some paper and a pencil nearby while you read. Write the headings as you come to them, and when you've read a section, jot down a brief summary of the main ideas. You don't have to be super-neat since these notes won't be turned in. But be sure you can read what you've written.

When you've finished, you will have an outline of the material contained in that chapter. Your notes will be arranged in the order the author used in writing. But you may find it helpful to arrange the words and phrases in a different pattern. On another sheet of paper you could write down a main idea and draw a circle around it. Then you could connect other related facts and ideas to it with lines and arrows.

However you arrange the information from the chapter, every time you write it down you help your mind remember it.

Make your own learning tools

You can take advantage of many learning methods by making and using flashcards. These cards are a great way to learn lists of information like vocabulary words and their definitions, math facts, or words in a foreign language.

Flashcards are easy to make out of 3×5-inch index cards. Write the "question" on one side and the "answer" on the other. For example, for a Spanish vocabulary card, the front would say "*azul*" and the back would say "blue."

Once you have a set of cards, you can use them in various ways. Go through them by yourself, one by one, checking the backs to make sure your answers are right. Set aside the ones you didn't know right away to go through a second time.

Or use the flashcards with a friend. As your friend holds up the cards, one at a time, you call out each answer. (Your friend can see the correct answers on the backs of the cards.) Take turns until you both know the material. And don't forget that you can flip the cards over and ask the questions the other way around.

For some students the very act of writing out the information may be the most helpful part of using flashcards. But for others, the repetition of saying the answers out loud or seeing the correct information flashed in front of their eyes will be the best memory aid.

You can probably think of many other ways to use the different methods of learning. Have you ever heard of a mnemonic device? It's a memory aid, usually a word or phrase that helps you remember a list or sequence. Here's a famous example: "Every good boy does fine." The first letters of these words are E G B D F, the notes of the lines in the treble clef in music. And who is ROY G. BIV? This name spells out the initials of the colors of the spectrum—red, orange, yellow, green, blue, indigo, and violet. You can make up your own mnemonic devices for other lists—what about a phrase to help you remember the order of the planets in our solar system?

Once you get started, you'll think up lots of creative ways to learn. You might make a map that's really a puzzle to help you remember where all the states are. Or you could create a skit using the foreign language vocabulary you're supposed to learn. You could even invent a board game to help you in one of your classes. Paint a piece of cardboard with a path for the markers to follow. Then make up a bunch of question cards—you could use questions about history facts, for example. When a player lands on a question square, he or she has to draw a card and answer the question correctly in order to move ahead. Let your imagination roam free and you'll no doubt come up with other creative learning tools.

No matter what you think your learning style is, it's a good idea to try a few different ones. Many people learn best using a combination of styles. And your style may change as you get older. So use a variety of learning methods to get the most out of your schoolwork.

5. Handling Homework

Even though you don't do it at school, homework is an important part of your schoolwork. It allows you to practice the things you learn in class—a set of math problems, for instance, might use the math ideas the teacher presented that day.

Homework also gives you a chance to do work that takes a lot of time. For example, you might read a chapter in your textbook for homework and then discuss it the next day in class. If you had to read it in school in addition to discussing it, you wouldn't be able to get as much done.

Preparing for tests is also a kind of homework. When you read over the chapters you'll be tested on or review the spelling words from the last few weeks, you may not think of it as homework. But in fact it is schoolwork that you are doing at home, even though your teacher may not have assigned it.

Other kinds of homework may be long-term projects. You might be asked to do research and write a paper that is due six weeks from now. Certainly you can't do the whole project the night before it's due. It's up to you to plan your time and get each stage of the "homework" done so your project will be ready when it should be.

Tools for school

In addition to the pencils and pens you need for class, a very important tool for school is a way of keeping your assignments and homework together and easy to find. How many times have you called a friend in a panic because you didn't know what the homework was? Of course you wrote it down, but you couldn't find the paper you wrote it on.

One way to make sure you always have the assignment is to write it in your notebook for that class. Do you keep your notes from science or social studies class in a spiral-bound or looseleaf notebook? Use that same notebook for each day's homework assignment as well.

The problem with using the small notebooks sold as assignment pads is that they can easily become separated from the rest of your books. By keeping all of the information for one class together—homework *and* class notes—you make it a lot easier for yourself. You can look over what's happened in class so far and review all the work you've done since the beginning of the year.

Both spiral-bound and looseleaf notebooks now come with pocket folders included. These are great for keeping all your handouts (the poem you have to memorize for language arts, the math problems that are due tomorrow, the map of major rivers to be learned for social studies) collected and available. It's hard to do your homework if you don't have the mimeographed sheet it's written on! A notebook with pockets will be a big help.

It's also hard to do your homework if you haven't written down the assignment correctly. Listen carefully when your teacher tells you what to do for the next day. Sometimes those directions will be different from the ones in the textbook. Maybe the book says you should only give "true" or "false" as answers to the questions at the end of the chapter. But your teacher wants everyone to write whole sentences explaining the answers as well. Which way of doing it will get a better grade? This is the kind of thing it's important to pay attention to.

Helpful hints for homework

Perhaps your teacher has already given you some suggestions for studying more effectively. Or maybe you've picked up an idea or two from watching how your friends do their homework. Here are some ways of dealing with your homework that you may not have thought of before.

Breaking up the job

When you have a large assignment to complete, separate it into smaller pieces. The idea of reading a long chapter of difficult science material may seem overwhelming to you. But if you break up the job into manageable segments, you'll feel more able to get started. Decide to read only the first one or two subsections; that will be the end of the job for now. Later (maybe after dinner or the next morning) you can read the next two subsections, and so on until the whole chapter is finished. Naturally, this only works if you have enough time to split up the assignment over a couple of days.

One reason this method works is that it makes the job look easier. After all, anyone can read just two short subsections of a chapter. If you take each piece at a time, you are more likely to get started.

Another way it helps is by allowing you enough time between segments to make sure you understand the material. You'll be able to think over the shorter part that you've finished before moving on to another section. Even quite difficult assignments become easier to grasp when you approach them like this.

This method of breaking up a job works for assignments other than reading. Think of your five-page term paper and all the research and writing it will require. You can separate the work into three major chunks: doing the research, making the outline, and writing the paper itself. Divide up the time you have until the paper is due, and enter the dates you plan to finish each work segment on your calendar. Attacking this kind of project in smaller bits will help get the job done on time.

Give yourself a treat

Why not give yourself a reward when you finish a hard assignment? Knowing that a treat is awaiting you often makes you more eager to get the job done. You might promise yourself a half hour of playing ball or watching TV. Or maybe you'll save the next chapter of that exciting novel or a telephone chat with a friend until after you've done your math homework.

Rewards actually work, and you know best what will make you get busy. Just be sure that the treat you promise yourself isn't more than the job deserves. Watching TV for two hours is way too big a reward for completing a fifteen-minute spelling review. And don't get in the habit of using sweets or junk food to treat yourself—they're not good for either your brain or your body.

Use a timer

Do you try to do all of your math homework at one sitting and find that your brain is bogging down before you're finished? Maybe you'd be better off with a timer. Some people find that they concentrate best for a short period of time, like half an hour.

Why not see if it works for you? Set the kitchen timer for half an hour and then settle down with whatever assignment you plan to work on. When the bell rings, stop what you are doing and mark your place. Now take a five-minute break to stretch and clear your mind before going back to work. You may find that this short pause renews your energy and enthusiasm so that you can work efficiently for another half hour.

Another way to do timed homework is to change to another kind of assignment after your five-minute break. If you've been doing math problems, start on your reading for social studies for the next half hour. And you might even want to move on to review for your science quiz for a third half hour before returning to the math. Mixing the types of work and fields of study often will help your mind stay alert.

At first glance, this way of studying may sound confusing. But many students find that it is an effective method of staying on top of their homework. It is especially useful in dealing with jobs that really have no end, like studying foreign language vocabulary or reviewing for a test. You could keep working on either one of these all night. Using a timer lets you know when you've done enough, at least for now.

Use a list

Are you someone who takes a lot of pleasure in finishing something and crossing it off your list? If so, using a timer method of doing your homework will probably make you want to tear out your hair.

For some students, completing an assignment feels like a reward all by itself. If you are one of these people, make a list of your homework each day so that you can keep track of what has to be done. Just make sure that you don't load your list up so much that there is no possibility of doing it all. And it's still a good idea to take a break from time to time. When you find yourself slowing down or feeling drowsy, jog around the block or play on the floor with the cat for a change of pace.

What about open-ended jobs? If the idea of using a timer to decide how long to review for a quiz or study your vocabulary words doesn't appeal to you, here are some other possibilities. You can decide in advance how many times you will go through your list of definitions or whatever. When you've done it as many times as you've decided on, that job is finished. Cross it off your list and move on to the next assignment.

Another way to handle open-ended work is to test yourself. Let's say you are memorizing the names of U.S. presidents and the dates they held office. Go over the information a number of times until you feel you know it, and then try to write the names and dates on a blank piece of paper. If you can do it with no more than one or two mistakes, you're ready for the test in class.

Do the hard stuff or the easy stuff first?

Whatever works best for you is the right answer to this question. Some people believe that the best way to study is to work on a hard subject first. Then working on an easier subject afterward is sort of like a reward. These people hate knowing that the hard stuff is sitting there waiting for them. They like to get it over with first.

Other people feel strongly that beginning with a topic that's easy for them is a better way to work. It puts them in the studying mood and makes them feel ready to tackle harder subjects. Besides, they like being able to cross one assignment off their lists even if it's something easy.

You might want to try each of these methods and see if one works better for you. Maybe you'll be surprised at how much more you accomplish.

Working alone or working with others

Whether you decide to work on a particular project by yourself or with others often depends on the assignment. It also depends on the kind of person you are. Some students prefer wrestling with homework problems by themselves. They may be worried that others will think they're stupid if they don't catch on to everything right away. Or students may find they're tempted to chat instead of work when they do homework with friends.

Others don't feel comfortable facing a pile of work all alone. They can get on with their assignments better if there are other people around. Sometimes being in a situation where a number of people are also working helps these students get going on their own assignments.

Maybe you already know from experience that you and your best friend don't do much homework when you're together. Even though you both plan to work, you end up just fooling around. But perhaps when you try to work by yourself, you seem to spend all your time sharpening your pencils or staring into space. Why not try studying in the library? Everyone around you will also be working, but it's not a place where you can giggle and goof off.

Some projects really are best done alone. It's hard to imagine how you could share reading an assigned chapter or writing a term paper with someone else. On the other hand, studying a foreign language or math facts by using flashcards works very well with a friend.

Look it over one more time

Some homework does not have to be written, like reviewing for a quiz or reading a chapter in your textbook so that you are ready to discuss it the next day. That is the kind of homework you carry to school with you in your head. But other homework is meant to be written out—like your math problems, or your essay for language arts, or your report for social studies.

It is a good idea to look over written homework one last time before you put your studying away for the evening. Homework needs to be neat enough for the teacher to read easily. It doesn't have to be absolutely perfect, with no cross-outs, unless your teacher says so. But it should look as if you care enough to do a good job. Don't forget that your teacher has a number of homework assignments to grade, and it's always more pleasant to look at work that is neatly done.

Check your homework for mistakes before taking it to school to turn in. If you are careful to line up the columns in your math problems, you will make fewer errors. Also, look up the spelling of words you're not sure of so that they are correct. (Here's a tip: If you know spelling is your weak point, try reading your homework paper backward, looking carefully at each word. You won't slide over so many errors that way.)

It's a good idea to gather up all your homework and schoolbooks before you go to bed at night so that they will all be in one place in the morning. It's easy to forget an important piece of homework in the morning when you are rushing to get to school on time.

Knowing that you've done all your homework to the best of your ability gives you a good feeling as you start your day. You'll be ready to participate in class discussions with enthusiasm, and if you have a test, you'll be able to tackle it with confidence.

6. Get a Head Start on Tests

When your teacher announces that a test is coming up, how do you feel? Do you look at tests as exciting challenges, or does the thought of one send you into a panic?

Many students are nervous about taking tests. Sometimes it's because they're afraid they don't completely understand the material or haven't studied it enough. But even students who feel sure they know the stuff they'll be tested on often get worried and upset when a test looms on the horizon.

A test is merely a way of finding out how much of the class material you have learned. And to do your best on a test, it pays to be prepared.

Preparing for tests

You've been doing your homework all along, so you'll be in pretty good shape when test time rolls around. That's a big help, because what your parents and teachers tell you really is true. You can't learn a whole unit by trying to cram all the information into your head in one night. Doing homework as it is assigned gives you time to think through the material from class and see how it all goes together to make sense.

Nevertheless, almost all students need to do some extra studying to prepare for tests. What's the best method of doing it? Of course, you can reread all the material, but that's often not necessary. If you have been doing well on your homework and have been able to understand the class discussions, here's one way to approach test preparation.

Page through the whole section of your textbook that the test will cover. Read the introduction, if there is one, to remind yourself of the "main idea." Then move on, reading only the headings and subheadings. Turn each one into questions and think about how you would answer them. For instance, if a heading is "The French Explore the New World," you might ask yourself, "Who were the important French explorers? When did they come to the New World? What part of the New World did they explore?"

If you can answer these questions, go on to the next heading. If you're not sure, read this section of the text to remind yourself.

Perhaps you have notes that you took in class. Now is the time to read them over, but don't simply skim through them. Stop and think about what questions your teacher asked during the class discussion. This helps you focus on the important points, and it might even give you an idea of what kinds of questions could be on the test.

How else can you prepare for a test? Try looking through the homework papers from this study unit. As you read them, you may remember more ideas or facts to fit into your overall understanding of the material.

Reviewing homework papers is especially useful when you're studying for a math test. You can try working two or three problems from each page of homework—be sure to cover up the answers as you work. If you find you have trouble with certain kinds of problems, you can practice doing a few more of them.

For spelling and foreign language vocabulary tests, use the lists of words that were handed out or get out your flashcards. Ask a friend or a family member to help you review. Put a pencil mark on the list beside any words you don't know, or set aside those flashcards to go over again.

When you use these review techniques, getting ready for a test takes less time. You'll feel confident that you've focused on the important material and that you're well prepared for the questions.

Get a head start

One of the best ways you can help yourself do well on tests is to make sure that you feel rested and alert. You've probably heard a million times that you should get a good night's sleep before a test, and the reason you've heard it so often is that it's true! Staying up late to study for a test rarely helps. Your brain is unlikely to retain much so late at night, and the next day you'll be slowed down and exhausted just when you need to be your peppiest.

You'll probably gather up your school stuff and put it somewhere handy the night before so you can snatch it up as you leave for school. But did you ever think of deciding ahead of time what clothes you'll wear on test day? It may sound like a weird idea if you don't do it already, but why not give it a try?

It's important to wear comfortable clothes when you're taking a test. After all, you want to be able to concentrate on the test questions, not on the waistband that's too tight or the sweater that itches around your neck. But don't wear your oldest and grubbiest outfit. One of the things that helps most on test day is a feeling of confidence; wearing something you look good in makes you feel this way.

Many students are nervous on the morning of a big test. If that's what happens to you, looking good and having your stuff all ready to go will let you relax a little. Get up early enough so you won't have to rush. Being in your seat in plenty of time will help you get set to do your best. And don't forget to eat a good breakfast. Both your body and your brain need food.

Use your head

At last you're sitting at your desk—well prepared, rested, and ready to go. You're probably tempted to grab your pencil and plunge in. But wait! Here are a few tips that can be useful no matter what kind of test you are taking.

Think ahead

First of all, glance through the whole test to see how long it is and what kinds of questions are in it. This preview gives you a chance to see what's coming; maybe there's an essay question at the end or a whole bunch of fill-in-the-blank sentences.

Looking over the test also lets you plan your

time so you don't spend too long on any one section. For example, if you have half an hour for the whole test, you don't want to spend twenty-eight minutes on the multiple-choice part and leave yourself only two minutes for an essay question. And don't forget that you'll want a few minutes at the end to go back and check your work. Try to allow this time so you can correct any careless mistakes before you hand in the test. A quick look through the whole thing before you get started is a good test-taking trick that can put you ahead of the game.

Get the message

Another useful idea is to read the test directions carefully before you pick up your pencil and begin marking your answers. This may seem obvious, but many students are so anxious to get going that they don't take time for this important step. Nothing makes you feel worse than to do poorly on a test you knew the answers to just because you didn't follow the instructions correctly. Take a couple of minutes at the start of each section of the test to think through what you're supposed to do. It will be time well spent.

Start off easy

Unless your teacher tells you otherwise, there's no law that says you have to answer the test questions in order. So why not do the easy ones first?

First of all, writing down the answers you're sure of is bound to make you more confident. Knowing you've already answered some questions correctly gives you the feeling that you're on the way, moving full speed ahead.

In addition, as you answer those easy questions you'll be reminded of other facts that will help you answer the hard ones. This isn't so surprising—your test probably covers only one unit or topic, and all the information you've learned is related. So instead of letting your brain come to a halt when you're stumped by a difficult question, just keep going. Then, when you go back to that tough problem, the right answer will probably pop right into your mind.

Doing the easy questions first also means that at least the answers you're sure of will be written down. This is nice to know in case you didn't plan quite right and you run out of time.

Make your answers clear

Neatness on tests can make a big difference. Some students mistakenly believe that if they write sloppily enough, their teacher will think that unreadable scrawl actually is the right answer. But, in fact, answers a teacher can't read get marked wrong. So take care to make your work easily understandable. That way your correct answers will get full credit.

What if you make a mistake in answering one of the questions? This happens to everyone from time to time. Of course you'll want to change it. Just be sure that your new answer can be read clearly. Either completely erase the original answer or totally cross it out. If you simply write one number or letter on top of the other, your teacher will have to be a mind reader to know which one you meant.

Don't give up

Once you've written in all the answers you're pretty sure of, go back to the beginning of the test and look at the questions that had you stumped. Maybe by now you've come up with answers to some of them. But there might be a few that you still can't figure out. Unless your teacher has told you not to, go ahead and make a guess. After all, there's always a chance that you'll be right. And once you've read the tips on various kinds of questions in the next chapter of this book, your chances of guessing right will be even better.

7. Tackling Tests

Naturally, the best way to do well on tests is to study hard enough so that you can answer the test questions correctly. Tests are designed to measure how much of the subject you have learned. But even when you do know the material, some test questions can be difficult to answer. Don't despair—there are ways of figuring out how to deal with those tough questions.

True–false questions

In a true–false question, you read a statement and have to decide whether it's true or not. Even if you're sure of your facts, be on the lookout for words like *never, always, every,* and *none.* These are "danger words" that should make you stop and think carefully before marking your answer. A statement containing a danger word is usually false because these words mean there are no exceptions. For example, is this statement true or false:

All kids love ice cream.

Maybe you don't know anyone who doesn't like ice cream, but somewhere in the world there's sure to be at least one kid who hates it. If the statement said "Most kids love ice cream," it would be true.

In the same way, be careful of statements that give causes or reasons. If it sounds as if it is the *only* reason for something, the statement is probably false. Here's an example:

When a dog barks, it is because he is angry.

This statement is clearly false. A dog might bark because he is happy, or lonely, or for some reasons we don't even know about. We can turn this into a true statement by saying, "When a dog barks, it may be because he is angry."

Remember there are *some* statements that *are* true even though they contain one of the danger words. You know, for instance, that "All circles are round" is a true statement. So think each question through as you take a true–false test, and be certain that you know what each statement really means.

Here's one more tip from the experts who study how tests are made. They say that there are usually more true statements than false ones in a test. This means that if you have to guess, you're probably better off marking the statement "true."

Multiple-choice questions

These are either incomplete statements followed by a number of possible endings or questions with a list of possible answers. You have to choose which ending or answer is correct.

Often you can pick out the right answer immediately. But if not, don't waste time searching for the one that's correct. Instead, narrow the field by getting rid of the choices you know are wrong. How can you do this?

Answers that are likely to be wrong

As in true–false questions, you can usually assume that an answer with a "danger word" is wrong. Words like *all, none, everybody,* and *nobody* in an answer should make you think about eliminating that choice. What "danger word" answer can you eliminate from the example below?

> The reason most Americans eat turkey on Thanksgiving is that
> a. everybody likes turkey.
> b. turkeys have carunculate heads.
> c. turkeys say "gobble, gobble."
> d. turkey is the traditional main dish.

If you decided *a* was wrong, you were right!
Now take a look at choice *b.* You probably

don't know what "carunculate" means. (It refers to the wattles that hang down under a turkey's beak.) Even if you had been studying Thanksgiving and turkeys in school, it is likely that "carunculate" would be a word you'd never seen before. When you see a completely unfamiliar word or phrase, you can almost always get rid of that choice. Teachers don't expect students to know information that wasn't in the material they studied.

In this example choice *b*, all by itself, is a true statement—turkeys *do* have heads with wattles on them. But this is not the reason most people eat turkey on Thanksgiving. So even though it's true, it's not the right answer, and you can eliminate it.

Now that you've rejected two of the four choices, is there another one you can get rid of? It's a safe bet that a totally ridiculous or jokey answer is not the right one. So choice *c* can't be correct. And that leaves you with answer *d*.

You probably knew the correct answer the moment you finished reading this question about turkey. It was pretty obvious that three of the choices were wrong. But they are good examples of the kinds of answers you might find in a multiple-choice test. Keep your eyes open for choices that contain "danger words," words you've never run across in your studying, and silly suggestions. Once you've eliminated these possibilities, you may often find that you're left with only one answer—the right one.

In multiple-choice questions involving numbers, there's another trick you can try. Experts have found that the largest and smallest numbers are usually choices you can eliminate. For some reason, people who make up tests tend to surround the correct answer with wrong answers that are higher and lower. Try this question and see how you do:

> How many feet are in a mile?
> a. 528
> b. 5,280
> c. 52,800
> d. 528,000

Assuming you don't know the answer, at least you can eliminate choices *a* and *d*. Now you have one chance in two of guessing right instead of one chance in four. And sometimes just getting rid of a couple of the possible choices makes it easier to think about the ones that are left. Did you figure out that *b* is the correct answer, or was it a lucky guess?

Answers that are likely to be right

Just as there are ways to eliminate wrong answers for some questions, there are ways to pick out the correct answers for certain kinds of multiple-choice questions. One of these is to see if there are two similar-looking answers in your group of choices. If so, it is probable that one of them is correct. Once again, narrowing the possibilities down to two choices won't tell you which of those two is the right answer. But at least you've given yourself a better chance to make a correct guess. Take a look at the following question:

> Which explorer is known for conquering the Aztec people in Mexico?
> a. Joliet
> b. Hudson
> c. Cortez
> d. Coronado

Obviously the names Cortez and Coronado look a lot alike. And once you've gotten that far, maybe you'll remember that the man who conquered the Aztecs was Cortez.

Another type of question to look for is one where a choice is "all of the above." This, too, tends to be a correct answer. And if you're pretty sure that two of the other choices are correct, you'll know you should pick "all of the above." Take a look at this example:

> Which of these foods is high in calcium?
> a. milk
> b. cheese
> c. broccoli
> d. all of the above

Let's say you know that both milk and cheese have plenty of calcium, but you're not too sure about broccoli. Don't waste time worrying about the broccoli. Since you can choose only one answer, you have to take the one that includes both milk and cheese.

Don't expect magic

Keep in mind that these tricks for choosing right answers won't work all the time. There are lots of questions that don't follow these patterns. And if these tricks were foolproof, everyone could get perfect test scores every time.

There's no substitute for studying, and there's nothing more satisfying than doing well on a test because you really understand the material you've worked hard to learn. But even if you are completely prepared for a test, you may feel nervous about it. And, like anyone else, you may run across a question you can't answer. These techniques will give you a way of getting started on tough questions.

Fill in the blanks

This is a very common kind of test question, and when you come across one, there's no way you can guess at the answer successfully. After all, you're not just taking a chance on one of two or one of four possibilities—you're picking a word out of the air.

However, you can often find a clue by reading the whole sentence. Can you tell what kind of word is needed to complete it? If you can, you'll be more likely to figure out the correct fill-in answer. Try this one:

Columbus first sailed from _____
to the New World in the year
_____.

It's pretty obvious that the second blank needs a date (1492) to complete it. Did you figure out that the first blank needs the name of a country? Most fill-in questions aren't quite this easy, but they do contain clues to the kind of word you should be looking for.

After you've filled in all the blanks, read each sentence over again to make sure your answer makes sense.

Matching lists

In this kind of question there are two lists, and you have to match each item from one list with an item from the other. You either draw lines to connect the matching pairs or write the correct letter or number next to each item in one of the lists.

Looking at two lists of words or phrases can be kind of confusing even if you know all the material you're being tested on. Here's a good way to reduce your confusion. Start by looking at the top item on one of the lists; cover up the rest of that list with your hand or a piece of blank paper. Now you can concentrate on choosing the item from the other list that matches best with the word you're working on, and you won't get distracted by all the others.

Here's a sample to try:

1. reservation   a. built earthworks east of the Mississippi River

2. caribou   b. land set aside for Indians

3. Eskimos   c. home of the Shoshone

4. buffalo   d. food for the Eskimos

5. Mound Builders   e. hunted on the Great Plains

6. Great Basin   f. last Indian group to come to North America

It's often easier to start with a definition and look through the other column for the word that's being defined. So take a look at item *a*. You can tell that the answer must be a group of people, not a place or a kind of animal. But is it "Eskimos" or "Mound Builders"? If you're not sure, the word "Builders" gives you a clue that these people probably were the ones who "built" earthworks, so *a* matches with 5.

Now look at *b*—this one is pretty easy, and you shouldn't have much trouble matching it with "reservation." And when you go on to *c*, the only place name on the first list is "Great Basin," so you can match up *c* with 6. (If you hadn't already used "reservation," you might think it is the answer for "home of the Shoshone." But if you matched up *1* and *c*, you wouldn't have a definition for "reservation," so you can decide that the way you have answered must be correct.)

When you've gotten this far, the rest is easy. The word that matches "food for the Eskimos" has to be either "caribou" or "buffalo." But you probably remember that buffalo lived on the Great Plains, and caribou lived farther north in what is now Canada and Alaska, so you know which answer is correct. And the last two answers are obvious—even if you hadn't studied at all, you'd know that the last Indian group to come to North America must be "Eskimos," not "buffalo."

Did you notice that item *e* is a little bit tricky? If you had started with that phrase, you might have thought the answer should be the name of an Indian tribe, not an animal. Now that you've filled in the other answers, of course, you can see that it means the buffalo were hunted on the Great Plains. And when you stop to think about it, you know that neither the Mound Builders nor the Eskimos (the two groups of Indians in the list) lived on the Great Plains. But this is a good example of how you can get confused if you don't take time to look over the whole question.

Be sure to read the directions for matching-list questions carefully so you'll know what you're supposed to do. For instance, sometimes the two lists have the same number of items so that each one matches up with only one from the other list. But sometimes one list has more items than the other. Are you supposed to use one item twice, or is there an item that won't be used? Don't go crazy trying to guess about this—find out before you start.

Essay questions

Many students dread the idea of answering an essay question. They seem to think it's much harder than other kinds of test questions. An essay question does take more time to answer, and you have to think through what you're going to write. But really, writing a short essay gives you a chance to show how well you've learned the material for the class. And it's the only time you get to express your own opinion on a test—that can be a lot of fun!

As in the other sections of a test, it's important to read the instructions for an essay question carefully. You need to know exactly what is required in your answer. For instance, look at this question: "Which country contributed most to the exploration of the New World? Give reasons for your answer." It won't be enough simply to write down the name of a country in your answer—you have to explain why you chose that one.

In a question like this, it's up to you to decide what you think is the best answer. You might think Spain contributed most, or England, or maybe France. What facts do you know that back up this opinion? Your answer is based on the material you've studied in class and in homework assignments. When you write your essay, you will have to use the facts you've learned to support the opinion you are giving.

Four steps to success

There's no secret to writing a good answer to an essay question. Just follow these four steps:

1. *Think through what you want to say* in your essay. It's worth taking time to get your ideas organized in your mind before you start writing, even if your answer will be only one paragraph.

2. *Jot down quick notes* or a very brief outline on the back of your test paper—this keeps you from forgetting what you've planned to say.

3. *Write your answer in complete sentences and state things as clearly as you can.*

Pretend you are explaining your ideas to someone who knows nothing at all about the subject. This helps to keep you from leaving important information out.

4. *Try to finish in time to read over your essay* before the bell rings. It's easy to leave out letters or whole words when you're writing a test answer, and you'll want to fix up any mistakes so your teacher won't have trouble knowing what you meant to say.

Before you hand it in

Whatever kind of test you're taking, it's a good idea to go back and check your paper before you hand it in. You may find answers that are too sloppy to be read; you may find questions you forgot to answer; you may find careless errors that need to be corrected. Now is the time to fix all these little problems. It's even possible that as you go through your test one more time, you'll suddenly come up with an answer you couldn't remember earlier.

But what if, no matter how well you tried to plan things, time is up and you haven't finished the test? There are still some questions you didn't get to, or you're in the middle of writing your essay. What should you do?

First of all, write on your test, "I ran out of time here." This won't improve your test score, but at least it will let your teacher know why you didn't answer all the questions. And if this happens on more than one test, it's probably something you should discuss with your parents and your teacher. Maybe there is a way you can take your tests without a time limit. Some schools now allow students to do this, and it's worth asking about if you have a lot of trouble finishing your tests on time.

If you're in the middle of an essay question when time runs out, it's a good idea to also jot down an outline for the rest of your answer. This will take only a moment since you already have notes written down. Copy them quickly at the end of your paper so the teacher will know what you planned to say to complete your essay.

What's a test for, anyway?

Do you still feel nervous when you think about taking tests? Remember that the only purpose of a test is to measure how much you've learned about a particular subject. Your teacher isn't trying to trick you or trap you with impossible questions. So if you've done your homework and paid attention in class, you'll do fine on your test.

8. Make It Easy on Yourself

Is there anything else that can help you do your best work in school? Yes, there is, and this may surprise you—it's your attitude.

When you think about it, it makes sense that your attitude toward school plays an important part in how much you get out of it. If you're enthusiastic and cheerful in class, your classmates and your teacher are likely to "catch" your positive outlook.

On the other hand, if all you do is talk about how "boring" everything in school is, you're not giving yourself a chance to find school interesting and even exciting. Maybe your schoolwork is "boring" because you think it's going to be boring before you even start. Why not try a new approach? After all, you have to go to school whether you want to or not, so you might as well make it as much fun as you can!

How can you tell if you have a good attitude in class? One of the most important things is participation. Do you speak up in class discussions? Some students are embarrassed to say anything in front of the whole class. They think they'll sound stupid or they'll stumble over their words. It doesn't help much to have someone say, "Don't be so shy." But it does help to remember that at least half of your classmates feel the same way you do. They'll admire your bravery in contributing to discussions. And the teacher will be pleased to have more people adding their thoughts and ideas—it makes class more interesting.

As for sounding stupid, have you ever heard that "The only stupid question is the one you don't ask"? That's a roundabout way of saying that it's stupid *not* to ask a question if you don't understand something. And it's true. Chances are that if you are confused about something, you're not the only one in class who feels that way. It's much better to raise your hand and ask for an explanation now. That way you won't be completely mystified by everything that follows.

Participating by joining in class discussions and by asking questions when you're not sure what's going on not only helps you keep up with class work, it also makes the time you spend in class more enjoyable. In addition, it lets the teacher know you're paying attention. This is important. Teachers spend a lot of time preparing for their classes, and they're only human. They get annoyed when they feel no one is bothering to listen.

What else do teachers find annoying? You probably already know the answer. The same kinds of things that make your parents crazy make teachers tear their hair out too. So if you want to get the most out of school with the least fuss and bother, here are some things you shouldn't do:

• showing off how smart you are—this is also known as having a smart mouth;

• pushing, shoving, and acting rowdy in class—save it for the playground and for your friends who will appreciate it;

• being late and/or unprepared for class—this shows how little you care about your schoolwork;

• making up feeble excuses for lateness or for doing poorly on tests—no one likes to listen to whining, and besides, that creative streak can be put to better use in your work for class.

You know from your own experience that it's more fun to do things with someone who's enthusiastic and who seems to be enjoying whatever is going on. Your teacher feels the same way. Try volunteering the next time a class project comes up. You may discover that it's a lot more interesting than you expected, and it will let your teacher know that you're doing more than just sleeping through class.

But what if you try your best to be cheerful and cooperative and you still feel your teacher doesn't like you? Sometimes this happens. There are people whose personalities just don't seem to go together very well, and you may be in one of those situations.

Probably you won't be able to change to another class, so it's best to make up your mind to put up with it for this year. Next year things will no doubt be better. And there are things you can do to make this school year more pleasant.

First of all, think about how you act in class. Is there something you're doing—chewing your gum noisily, interrupting other people, or whatever—that irritates your teacher horribly? It may not be really obvious, but if your teacher has said, "One more sarcastic comment from you and it's curtains," you should have a clue to what's annoying him or her. Maybe you can change your behavior in this one area, and when your teacher sees that you're trying, it will make things a lot better.

Another way to improve things is to ask your teacher for help with something you don't understand. Naturally, this is the right step whenever you have a problem in any of your classes, but it can be very hard to do if you feel a teacher doesn't like you. However, get your nerve up and ask the teacher for an appointment either before or after school.

When you get there, explain what it is that you're having trouble with, and be prepared to listen carefully. It isn't easy to take this first step, but try hard not to be nervous or afraid. You may be surprised at how kind your teacher can be. And once you've made it clear that you want to do the best you can in the class, it's likely that things will improve.

What if you have a different kind of problem? You get along fine with your teacher, but you're falling behind in your schoolwork. You try as hard as you can, but you just can't seem to keep up. What should you do?

The first thing to remember is, it's not your fault. If you've really been trying to do your schoolwork and you just can't get a grasp on it, maybe you're going about it the wrong way. You may feel embarrassed or ashamed that you're having trouble. But it probably won't do much good to just keep trying harder by yourself. You need some help.

Have you had a conference with your teacher? Maybe there is some little piece of information you missed when you were sick with the flu. Or maybe it's something more basic that you need assistance with. Sitting down with the teacher and working through the problem area can make it clear to both of you what you're doing wrong. And once you get it straightened out, you'll be back on track.

Sometimes problems aren't so easily solved, but don't give up. Keep looking for help. Maybe you need to talk to your parents or an older brother or sister. They care about you, and since they know you so well they may be able to spot the problem in the way you're thinking about your schoolwork. And if they can't figure it out, they'll be able to find someone who can.

School isn't just a matter of getting good grades. It's the place where you spend a lot of your time and where you see your friends. Maybe you joke around and say that gym and recess are your favorite subjects. But did you ever think that math and science and social studies and language arts are gym class for your mind? And doing well on a test is just as exciting as scoring the winning goal in a game. Schoolwork can be a lot of fun if you give yourself a chance!

Index

Elizabeth James and Carol Barkin are the coauthors of over two dozen books for young readers, including several successful books of advice for students: *How to Write a Term Paper, How to Write a Great School Report,* and *How to Write Your Best Book Report.*

Elizabeth James attended Colorado College and received a B.A. in mathematics. She has written screenplays and nonfiction and novels for adults. She lives in Beverly Hills, California.

Carol Barkin received a B.A. in English from Radcliffe College. Formerly a full-time editor of children's books, she now does editorial work when she's not writing. She lives in Hastings-on-Hudson, New York.

Ms. James and Ms. Barkin have been collaborators since 1975, when they worked on an educational magazine. Although living 3,000 miles apart, they continue to write books together, a challenge to their organizational skills.